CORE LIBRARY OF US STATES

Tennessee

BY ANNIE BRIGHT
CONTENT CONSULTANT
Pamela Bobo
Instructor of History
Tennessee State University

Core Library
An Imprint of Abdo Publishing
abdobooks.com

abdobooks.com

Published by Abdo Publishing, a division of ABDO, PO Box 398166, Minneapolis, Minnesota 55439. Copyright © 2023 by Abdo Consulting Group, Inc. International copyrights reserved in all countries. No part of this book may be reproduced in any form without written permission from the publisher. Core Library™ is a trademark and logo of Abdo Publishing.

Printed in the United States of America, North Mankato, Minnesota.
052022
092022

Cover Photos: Shutterstock Images, map and icons; Olga Zakharova/Shutterstock Images, guitar, microphone, hat, boot
Interior Photos: Will Zheng/Shutterstock Images, 4–5; Kevin Ruck/Shutterstock Images, 7; Red Line Editorial, 9 (Tennessee), 9 (USA); Shutterstock Images, 10, 19 (flag), 19 (tree); Matt Hamilton/Chattanooga Times Free Press/AP Images, 12–13; North Wind Picture Archives/AP Images, 16; Matthew L. Niemiller/Shutterstock Images, 19 (salamander); Raul Baena/Shutterstock Images, 19 (bird); Mark J. Barrett/Alamy, 19 (horses); Bettmann/Getty Images, 20, 43; Melinda Fawver/Shutterstock Images, 22–23; Jo Crebbin/Shutterstock Images, 27; Corbis Historical/Getty Images, 28–29; Sean Pavone/Shutterstock Images, 33, 45; Ron Davis/Archive Photos/Getty Images, 34–35; Joe Hendrickson/Shutterstock Images, 37; Tatiana Volgutova/Shutterstock Images, 38

Editor: Katharine Hale
Series Designer: Joshua Olson

Library of Congress Control Number: 2021951556

Publisher's Cataloging-in-Publication Data

Names: Bright, Annie, author.
Title: Tennessee / by Annie Bright
Description: Minneapolis, Minnesota : Abdo Publishing, 2023 | Series: Core library of US states | Includes online resources and index.
Identifiers: ISBN 9781532197840 (lib. bdg.) | ISBN 9781098270605 (ebook)
Subjects: LCSH: U.S. states--Juvenile literature. | Southeastern States--Juvenile literature. | Tennessee--History--Juvenile literature. | Physical geography--United States--Juvenile literature.
Classification: DDC 976.8--dc23

Population demographics broken down by race and ethnicity come from the 2019 census estimate. Population totals come from the 2020 census.

CONTENTS

CHAPTER ONE
The Volunteer State 4

CHAPTER TWO
History of Tennessee 12

CHAPTER THREE
Geography and Climate 22

CHAPTER FOUR
Resources and Economy 28

CHAPTER FIVE
People and Places 34

Important Dates. 42

Stop and Think 44

Glossary. 46

Online Resources 47

Learn More 47

Index 48

About the Author. 48

CHAPTER ONE

THE VOLUNTEER STATE

Soldiers load a cannon with gunpowder. A boy in the crowd puts his fingers in his ears and closes his eyes. He knows a loud boom is coming. The soldiers scramble back from the cannon, and it fires. Many people in the crowd jump.

The crowd is watching a cannon demonstration at Shiloh National Military Park. The Battle of Shiloh in Tennessee was one of the deadliest battles of the American Civil War (1861–1865). Tennessee earned its nickname,

Shiloh National Military Park was founded in 1894 to honor the Civil War battle fought there.

PERSPECTIVES
KING OF THE WILD FRONTIER

Davy Crockett was born in Tennessee in 1786. During his lifetime he became a bigger-than-life frontiersman. He was a sharpshooter, hunter, and storyteller. He used his reputation to help his political ambitions. He was elected to the Tennessee legislature and later to the US House of Representatives. He also served in the Tennessee militia. Crockett was even considered as a candidate for the presidency. He did not end up running and became disillusioned with politics. Crockett set off from Tennessee with friends to explore Texas. Once there he joined the Texas Army fighting in the Mexican-American War. Crockett died in the Battle of the Alamo on March 6, 1836.

the Volunteer State, because it sent so many soldiers to fight in wars. The soldiers were volunteers. The government did not require them to fight. Tennessee first earned this nickname during the War of 1812. When the Mexican-American War (1846–1848) broke out, the US government asked for 2,800 soldiers from Tennessee. More than 30,000 responded. This solidified the state's nickname. More than 150,000 Tennessean

The Mississippi River separates Memphis, Tennessee, from Arkansas, *far right*.

troops fought in the Civil War. The volunteer tradition continues today as people volunteer in Civil War reenactments. These events help modern people understand what life was like in that war.

EXPLORING TENNESSEE

Tennessee is located in the southeastern United States. The state is long and narrow. Eight states in total border Tennessee. Tennessee is tied with Missouri for bordering the most states. Kentucky and Virginia border Tennessee to the north. Missouri lies to the northwest and Arkansas to the west. The Mississippi River creates Tennessee's western border. Georgia, Alabama, and Mississippi make up Tennessee's southern border. North Carolina borders the state to the east.

Nashville is the capital and largest city of Tennessee. It is well-known for country music. Other major cities are Memphis, Knoxville, and Chattanooga. Memphis is also known for music, but its history is in blues and rock and roll. Knoxville is one of the gateways to the Great Smoky Mountains National Park. Chattanooga is located in southeastern Tennessee on the shores of the Tennessee River.

There is much to see in the Volunteer State outside of

THE *GRAND OLE OPRY*

The *Grand Ole Opry* is a country music radio show that began in 1925. At first it was called the *WSM Barn Dance*. The first performer was fiddle player Uncle Jimmy Thompson. The broadcast moved from the WSM studio to auditoriums. Some of its early performers included country music superstars such as Roy Acuff in 1938, Minnie Pearl in 1940, and Dolly Parton in 1969. In 1974 the *Opry* moved to its newly built Grand Ole Opry House. Established country music performers as well as newcomers continue to perform there. Their live performances are broadcast to millions of listeners.

MAP OF
TENNESSEE

Tennessee has many important cities and landmarks. How does this map help you understand all that Tennessee has to offer?

Many country stars have performed on the Grand Ole Opry House stage.

big cities. People can explore mountains, farmland, and more. Visitors can see horse ranches, cotton fields, and the rolling Mississippi River. There is something to interest everyone in Tennessee.

STRAIGHT TO THE SOURCE

During World War I (1914–1918), Corporal Alvin York of Tennessee almost single-handedly took out a group of German machine gunners. York was later awarded the Medal of Honor for his bravery. He wrote in his diary about the event:

> *There must have been over twenty [machine guns] and they kept up a continuous fire. Never letting up. . . . I had no time nohow to do nothing but watch them-there German machine gunners and give them the best I had. . . . At first I was shooting from a prone position; that is lying down; [just] like we often shoot at the targets in the shooting matches in the mountains of Tennessee; and it was [just] about the same distance. But the targets were bigger.*
>
> Source: Alvin York. *Sergeant York: His Own Life Story and War Diary.* Ebook, Racehorse Publishing, 2018.

CONSIDER YOUR AUDIENCE

Adapt this passage for a different audience, such as your younger friends. Write a blog post conveying this same information for the new audience. How does your post differ from the original text and why?

CHAPTER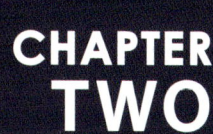

HISTORY OF TENNESSEE

The land that is now Tennessee has a long history. There is evidence that the first people in the area lived there approximately 11,000 years ago. These people were mostly nomadic hunters. Over thousands of years, people began planting crops and creating pottery. Some began building permanent settlements. By 900 CE, Mississippian Culture had become the dominant culture in Tennessee. The Mississippian peoples were ancestors of

Events such as the Green Corn Native American Festival & Powwow celebrate American Indian cultures in Tennessee.

CONQUISTADOR

Hernando de Soto was a conquistador, which translates to "he who conquers." Most of these early explorers came from Spain and Portugal. The conquistadores came to the Americas to make their fortunes. They searched for gold everywhere they traveled. They forced Indigenous people to guide them through the unknown lands. If any of the Indigenous people resisted, de Soto or the other conquistadores would kill the people and destroy their homes.

modern American Indian peoples. These include the Cherokee and Chickasaw Nations. Spanish explorer Hernando de Soto was the first European to encounter these peoples when he came to Tennessee in 1540.

De Soto and his men had come to America in search of gold. They were often violent toward American Indians. Europeans also brought diseases that killed many American Indians. The peoples that survived organized into nations still existing today. In addition to the Cherokee and Chickasaw peoples, the Choctaw, Creek, and Catawba peoples lived in Tennessee.

SETTLERS ARRIVE

By 1673 English and French traders had begun building trading posts. After the French and Indian War (1754–1763), land including modern-day Tennessee came under British control. The first permanent European settler in Tennessee, William Bean, built a cabin in northeastern Tennessee in 1769. More settlers soon joined him. This led to conflicts with American Indians already living there. When the Revolutionary War (1775–1783) began, Tennessee was not one of the 13 colonies. But it was still involved in the war. Many American Indian peoples sided with the British. They worried that American settlers would continue taking their lands. After the war, the US government punished American Indian peoples who sided with the British. The US government allowed settlers to take even more land.

Tennessee became the sixteenth state in 1796. More settlers arriving in the state led to increased conflict with American Indians. Similar conflicts occurred throughout the country. The US government responded

John Sevier became Tennessee's first governor in 1796.

with the Indian Removal Act of 1830. This allowed the government to forcibly remove American Indian peoples from their homelands. It was signed by President Andrew Jackson, who was from Tennessee. Beginning in 1838 the US government removed many American Indian peoples to what is now Oklahoma. This journey became known as the Trail of Tears. Thousands of American Indians died on the long, hard trip.

SLAVERY AND THE CIVIL WAR

By the mid-1800s, Tennessee was divided over the issue of slavery. Eastern Tennessee was largely against slavery. Western Tennessee was proslavery. Central Tennessee was divided. Central and western Tennessee had many plantations. Plantation owners relied on the forced labor of enslaved people. The whole country was facing the same debate. In 1861 war broke out. The southern slave states seceded from the United States, called the Union. They formed the Confederacy. Tennessee was the last state to secede. Many Eastern Tennesseans remained loyal to the Union.

PERSPECTIVES
AMERICAN INDIAN REMOVAL

The Indian Removal Act forced many American Indian peoples to relocate to Oklahoma. Many Cherokee people resisted removal. Eventually the US government forced them to leave. Chickasaw leaders sold land and paid for their own removal. They were able to control when they departed, which allowed them to escape some of the worst seasonal weather. Other people avoided removal entirely. Jobe Alexander's father went to Oklahoma on the Trail of Tears. Alexander said, "The last group that was rounded up revolted . . . and they made for hideaways in the mountains. That is why the Indians are back in North Carolina, Tennessee, and Georgia."

The Civil War was a bloody time during Tennessee's history. There were more than 1,400 battles and smaller skirmishes on Tennessee soil. An estimated 64,333 Confederate soldiers and 58,521 Union soldiers died in Tennessee during the Civil War.

RECONSTRUCTION AND BEYOND

The Civil War ended with the Confederacy's defeat. Tennessee was the first Confederate state to be readmitted to the Union on July 24, 1865. To rejoin the United States, Tennessee ratified the Thirteenth and Fourteenth Amendments to the US Constitution. These amendments outlawed slavery, granted citizenship to formerly enslaved people, and forbade states from preventing these people from voting.

The years after the Civil War are known as Reconstruction. It was a difficult time for former Confederate states. Plantation owners resented that slavery was no longer legal. Tennessee began passing Jim Crow laws. These state laws denied Black people

TENNESSEE
QUICK FACTS

Each US state has its own unique history and culture. How do Tennessee's state nickname and motto represent its history? Did you find any of Tennessee's state symbols surprising?

Abbreviation: TN
Nickname: The Volunteer State
Motto: Agriculture and commerce
Date of statehood: June 1, 1796
Capital: Nashville
Population: 6,910,840
Area: 42,144 square miles (109,152 sq km)

STATE SYMBOLS

State amphibian
Tennessee cave salamander

State horse
Tennessee walking horse

State bird
Mockingbird

State tree
Tulip poplar

19

On March 29, 1968, more than 200 striking sanitation workers took to the streets to protest poor working conditions. Memphis mayor Henry Loeb called in 4,000 National Guard troops.

many of the rights they had been promised by the federal government.

THE CIVIL RIGHTS MOVEMENT

The civil rights movement began in the 1950s as Black people and their allies fought against Jim Crow laws and other injustices. Huge protests happened in Memphis, Nashville, Knoxville, and Chattanooga. In 1968 Memphis sanitation workers went on strike to protest the city's mistreatment of its Black employees. Civil rights leader Martin Luther King Jr. came to offer his support. It was there that he was assassinated on April 4. King's death set off riots in more than 100 cities in the United States. Forty people died in those riots. The civil rights movement led to federal laws banning discrimination and protecting voting rights.

TENNESSEE GOVERNMENT

Like the US government, Tennessee's government has three branches. The executive branch is made up of state leaders, including the governor. The legislative branch writes and enacts the state's laws. The judicial branch is the court system. Though American Indian people live in Tennessee, the state has no federally recognized tribes.

FURTHER EVIDENCE

Chapter Two discusses Tennessee's state government. What was one of the main points of this section? What evidence is included to support this point? Read the article at the website below. Does the information on the website support the main point of the section? Does it present new evidence?

HOW STATE GOVERNMENT IS SET UP
abdocorelibrary.com/tennessee

CHAPTER THREE

GEOGRAPHY AND CLIMATE

Tennessee has three regions. They are East Tennessee, Middle Tennessee, and West Tennessee. The Great Smoky Mountains are in East Tennessee. The Smokies are part of the much bigger Appalachian Mountains. The Appalachians begin in southern Canada and end in central Alabama. East Tennessee's Cumberland Plateau is also part of the Appalachian Mountains.

The Lilly Bluff Overlook at the Obed Wild and Scenic River offers visitors stunning views of the Cumberland Plateau.

TENNESSEE WALKING HORSE

The Tennessee walking horse breed was first developed in Middle Tennessee using several different kinds of horses. The Tennessee walking horse has a distinctive way of moving. This horse breed moves smoothly across the ground in a flat-foot walk, running walk, or canter. Riders on Tennessee walking horses feel as if they are gliding over the ground. That means less jolting movement than a rider normally feels when riding a horse. These horses are also known for being gentle and kind. This makes the breed popular for trail rides and for work on ranches.

Middle Tennessee is mostly level with rolling hills. It's ideal for dairy farming and raising livestock. The region is known for its mules and horses, including the Tennessee walking horse. It is often called bluegrass country. The name *bluegrass* refers to both a kind of grass and a type of music. Both are found in the region.

West Tennessee is mostly flat. Bordered by the Mississippi and Tennessee Rivers, this region has rich soil. Most of the state's cotton is grown here.

CLIMATE

The climate in most of Tennessee is classified as humid subtropical. This means that summers are usually hot and humid, while winters are mild. This changes in the mountains, which generally are cooler.

Most of the state receives approximately 50 inches (127 cm) of precipitation each year. Snow is common in the mountains, where 10 inches (25 cm) or more is common in the winter. Snow is rarer but not impossible in the rest of the state, which can receive as much as 4 or 5 inches (10 or 13 cm) in a winter. The temperatures are mild enough that the snow quickly melts.

WILDLIFE

Differences in elevation affect the kinds of animals that live in Tennessee. Animals that live in the Great Smoky Mountains include red squirrels and spotted skunks. Peregrine falcons and saw-whet owls soar overhead. Approximately 1,500 black bears live in Great Smoky Mountains National Park.

PERSPECTIVES

DON'T FEED THE BEARS!

Black bears once roamed the entire state of Tennessee. By 1970 they were almost all gone due to hunting and habitat loss. Today they are slowly reclaiming their previous territories. Black bears usually avoid humans. But people often feed them on purpose. Others don't store their food and garbage properly. This means bears can access it. The bears become comfortable around humans. They can destroy property and cause other issues. Kim DeLozier is a wildlife biologist at Great Smoky Mountains National Park. He says, "The fundamental way we manage bears, for the most part, is to keep our food and our garbage away from black bears."

The Tennessee River and all of its tributaries form what is called a big river ecosystem. Birds fly over the riverbanks and surrounding land. Fish and turtles live in the streams. Mayfly larvae and crayfish live in the waters. They provide food for other animals.

Tennessee has the most known caves of any US state. The 9,600 caves are an ecosystem that houses hundreds of unique animal species. Ten bat species live in

Visitors to Great Smoky Mountains National Park might see wildlife such as elk.

these caves. Some of them are endangered. But others live in colonies that number in the thousands. Beetles, snails, and other small creatures live in the caves with the bats. The Tennessee cave salamander spends its entire life in the complete darkness of the caves.

EXPLORE ONLINE

Chapter Three discusses Tennessee's animals, including those in Great Smoky Mountains National Park. The article at the website below goes into more depth on this topic. Does the article answer any questions you have about Tennessee's animals? Does it provide new information?

EXPLORE: ANIMALS
abdocorelibrary.com/tennessee

CHAPTER FOUR

RESOURCES AND ECONOMY

Tennessee's economy was based almost entirely on agriculture until well into the 1900s. Cotton, tobacco, and livestock were the main products. These products remain part of Tennessee's agriculture industry today. Farmers grow cotton, soybeans, hay, tomatoes, tobacco, corn, and snap beans. Livestock products include chickens, eggs, cattle, milk, sheep, and horses. Forestry is another industry. Tennessee is a leading producer of hardwood lumber.

Tennessee's timber industry had a boom from the 1880s to the 1920s. It has remained a major industry since then.

THE BOLL WEEVIL

In Tennessee, it's illegal for people to plant cotton in their gardens. A small insect called the boll weevil is the reason why. The boll weevil nearly destroyed commercial cotton farms in the early and mid-1900s. The insects destroy cotton by feeding on the developing cotton bolls. Beginning in the 1970s, the US government worked to get rid of the insects. By 2009 Tennessee had finally managed to eradicate them. The government wanted to keep the boll weevil out of the state for good. It banned cotton in private gardens without a permit. This keeps people from accidentally bringing the insect back in cotton plants from other states.

FACTORIES AND ENERGY

There were a few textile- and iron-manufacturing plants in East Tennessee before 1900. Industrial growth in the 1930s and 1940s mostly came because of the new dams built to generate electricity. In 1933 the Tennessee Valley Authority began building a network of dams on the Tennessee River and its tributaries. These dams helped Tennessee's economy grow. World

War II (1939–1945) also increased industrial activity.

Manufacturing remains important to Tennessee's economy. Cars, machinery, chemicals, and rubber products are made in Tennessee. Different food and beverage items are also manufactured in the state.

OTHER INDUSTRIES

One of the fastest-growing industries in Tennessee

PERSPECTIVES
MINING IN TENNESSEE

Mining accounts for a small percentage of Tennessee's economy today. But it hasn't always been that way. In the 1840s geologist Gerard Troost recognized East Tennessee's mining and waterpower potential. He said, "Nature had stamped it as country for manufacturing." Deposits of more than 70 minerals and chemicals are scattered throughout the state. Iron ore was mined in the early settlement days. Coal mining began during the 1840s. The coal mined then and today is bituminous or soft coal. It's used for electricity and making steel. Other minerals mined in Tennessee include copper, zinc, phosphate, and ball clay.

is health care. Jobs for nurse practitioners, medical assistants, and other related medical positions grow each year. Other service positions such as welders, security guards, brick masons, and machine operators are also growing.

In 2019 tourism produced more jobs than any other industry in Tennessee. Visitors to Pigeon Forge can enjoy the Titanic Museum Attraction or the Dollywood theme park. Tourists can ride an elevator to the top of the Gatlinburg Space Needle. Families can visit the largest petting farm in Tennessee at Lucky Ladd Farms in Eagleville. As a state with beautiful parks, historical sites, and entertainment facilities, Tennessee has much to see.

The Gatlinburg Space Needle offers visitors a 360-degree view of Gatlinburg and the surrounding Great Smoky Mountains.

CHAPTER FIVE

PEOPLE AND PLACES

White people who are not Hispanic or Latino make up 73.5 percent of Tennessee's population. Seventeen percent of the state's population is Black, and 2 percent is Asian. Nearly 6 percent of Tennesseans are Hispanic or Latino. American Indian people make up 0.5 percent of the state's population. Tennessee's population has grown steadily since it was first recorded in the late 1700s.

Country singer Dolly Parton opened her Dollywood theme park in 1986. The park is a top tourist attraction in Tennessee.

Tennessee is home to many notable historical figures and celebrities. Singers Aretha Franklin and Miley Cyrus were both born in the state. Country singers Kelsea Ballerini and Kenny Chesney are from East Tennessee.

MEMPHIS

Memphis is located in southwestern Tennessee on bluffs above the Mississippi River. The city offers many attractions, including the home of rock and roll star Elvis Presley. The Graceland mansion welcomes more than 500,000 visitors each year. After the White House, it is the most famous private home in the United States.

The Memphis Grizzlies, a National Basketball Association team, play in Memphis. In addition, Memphis hosts golf championships and the Liberty Bowl football game. Memphis is also home to Saint Jude Children's Research Hospital. The hospital is world famous for its research and treatment of childhood cancer.

The *Grand Ole Opry*, recording studios, and record labels in Nashville helped it earn its nickname Music City.

MUSIC CITY

Nashville is often called Music City because of its long and vibrant history of music. It's also called the Home of Country Music. The *Grand Ole Opry*'s success led to the establishment of Music Row. Recording studios, record labels, entertainment offices, and other music businesses can be found within a few blocks of

Cayenne pepper gives Nashville hot chicken its spicy kick.

each other. In addition to country, the city is a hub for pop, rock, bluegrass, jazz, classical, blues, and soul music. Artists such as Taylor Swift, Ed Sheeran, and Kelly Clarkson have recorded albums in Nashville.

Nashville is also known for food. Nashville hot chicken is a signature dish, featuring spicy fried chicken on white bread with a pickle. Visitors to Nashville can also visit a replica of the Parthenon, a famous ancient structure in Athens, Greece.

EAST TENNESSEE

Much of East Tennessee is in or near the Appalachian Mountains. The way of life in these mountains and valleys has sometimes been seen as isolated. People of Appalachia have often had a hard life trying to make a living from the poor, rocky soil. But this area has a unique culture. The Museum of Appalachia is located in Clinton. It is a living history museum that tells stories of settlers

PERSPECTIVES

DOLLY PARTON

Dolly Parton is known worldwide for her success as a country music singer and songwriter. She based many of her songs on her childhood in the Smoky Mountains. Her first big break came when she joined the televised *Porter Wagoner Show* in 1967. Her musical success has continued since that time. Parton is also known for giving back. In 1995 she started her Imagination Library. The organization gives free books to children from birth to age five. In 2020 Parton donated $1 million for COVID-19 research. "I just felt so proud to have been part of that little seed money that will hopefully grow into something great and help to heal this world," she said.

in East Tennessee. It has one of the largest collections of Appalachian artifacts on display anywhere.

Knoxville was the state's first capital. It remained the capital until 1812. Today Knoxville is known for its good climate and low cost of living. Chattanooga is home to a Riverwalk that connects parks and historic districts. The Volunteer State has something for everyone. Nature lovers, music fans, and history buffs alike can find something to explore in Tennessee.

SEQUOYAH

Cherokee leader Sequoyah was born in 1775 in what is now Tennessee. He was raised by his mother and never learned to speak, read, or write English. As a young man Sequoyah became convinced that the Cherokee needed a written language. He began to develop a Cherokee syllabary, which is like an alphabet. Sequoyah assigned a symbol for each sound he heard in the Cherokee language. Soon a large number of Cherokee speakers learned to read and write using the syllabary. The syllabary can still be seen today on signs in northeast Oklahoma.

STRAIGHT TO THE SOURCE

The fiftieth anniversary of Martin Luther King Jr.'s assassination in Memphis was observed in April 2018. Professor Zandria Robinson spoke about the legacy of this event for Black people in Memphis today:

People in Memphis tend to wear their race on their sleeve. It's a very powerful, bold feeling: you're very aware of what your race is because of this legacy of King's assassination and the shadow in which we all live. I do find myself sometimes in a restaurant with my kid or partner, being the only Black people in there, and I just wonder, how . . . did this happen in our city with 600,000 people, about 400,000 of them African American?

Source: David Smith. "Memphis Died with Dr. King—Shadow of Civil Rights Leader Haunts City." *Guardian*, 1 Apr. 2018, theguardian.com. Accessed 9 Sept. 2021.

WHAT'S THE BIG IDEA?
Take a look at this passage. What connections does Robinson make between King's assassination and life in Memphis today?

IMPORTANT DATES

11,000 years ago
People first inhabit what is now Tennessee.

1540 CE
Hernando de Soto is the first European explorer to visit Tennessee.

1769
William Bean founds the first European settlement in Tennessee.

1796
Tennessee becomes the sixteenth US state.

1830
Andrew Jackson signs the Indian Removal Act. The US government forces American Indian peoples out of Tennessee.

1861
The Civil War begins. Tennessee secedes from the United States and joins the Confederacy.

1933
The Tennessee Valley Authority builds a network of dams on the Tennessee River and its tributaries.

1968
Martin Luther King Jr. is assassinated in Memphis on April 4. His death sets off riots in more than 100 US cities.

STOP AND THINK

Dig Deeper

After reading this book, what questions do you still have about Tennessee? With an adult's help, find a few reliable sources that can help you answer your questions. Write a paragraph about what you learned.

Why Do I Care?

Maybe you aren't a big fan of country or rock and roll music. But that doesn't mean you can't think about music's importance in Tennessee's culture. How does music affect your life? Were you surprised by some of the artists who have recorded in Nashville?

You Are There

Chapter Three discusses the many caves found in Tennessee. Imagine you are going on a hike into one of these caves. Write a letter to a friend at home about what you see on your hike. What do you notice about the animals that live there? Be sure to add plenty of detail to your letter.

Take a Stand

This book discusses Tennessee's two biggest cities, Nashville and Memphis. Which would you prefer to visit, and why?

GLOSSARY

assassinate
to kill an important person, often for political reasons

elevation
the height above sea level

Indigenous
relating to the earliest known residents of an area

larva
the immature, wingless, feeding stage of an insect

nomadic
having no set home but traveling from place to place, often with the seasons to find food

riot
the act of a group causing violence and disorder in public places

sanitation
related to hygiene and disease prevention through processes such as trash removal

secede
to leave a political union

skirmish
a minor fight in a war

tributary
a small stream or river that flows into and joins a larger one

ONLINE RESOURCES

To learn more about Tennessee, visit our free resource websites below.

Core Library CONNECTION
FREE! COMMON CORE MULTIMEDIA RESOURCES

Visit **abdocorelibrary.com** or scan this QR code for free Common Core resources for teachers and students, including vetted activities, multimedia, and booklinks, for deeper subject comprehension.

Booklinks NONFICTION NETWORK
FREE! ONLINE NONFICTION RESOURCES

Visit **abdobooklinks.com** or scan this QR code for free additional online weblinks for further learning. These links are routinely monitored and updated to provide the most current information available.

LEARN MORE

Harris, Duchess, and Kate Conley. *The Indian Removal Act and the Trail of Tears*. Abdo, 2020.

Kaminski, Leah. *Tennessee Volunteers*. Weigl, 2020.

INDEX

agriculture, 10, 13, 19, 24, 29, 30, 32
American Civil War, 5, 7, 16–18
American Indians, 13–16, 17, 21, 35, 40
Appalachian Mountains, 9, 23, 39

Bean, William, 15

caves, 26–27
Chattanooga, 8, 9, 20, 40
civil rights movement, 20–21, 41
Crockett, David, 6
Cumberland Plateau, 9, 23

dams, 30
de Soto, Hernando, 14

Great Smoky Mountains National Park, 8, 9, 25, 26, 27

Indian Removal Act of 1830, 15–16, 17

Jim Crow laws, 18–21

King, Martin Luther, Jr., 20–21, 41
Knoxville, 8, 9, 20, 40

manufacturing, 30–31
Memphis, 8, 9, 20, 36, 41

Mexican-American War, 6
mining, 31
music, 8, 24, 37–40

Parton, Dolly, 8, 39

Reconstruction, 18–19
rivers, 7–10, 24, 26, 30, 36

Sequoyah, 40
Shiloh National Military Park, 5, 9
slavery, 16–18

Tennessee walking horse, 19, 24

War of 1812, 6

About the Author

Annie Bright lives in Missouri, just one state over from Tennessee. She enjoys traveling and visiting beautiful places around the country.